I0489551

LY REVISED AND UPDATED EDITION

AFFILIATE SECRETS

E UNDERGROUND PLAYBOOK

ING AND CONNECTING WITH PEOPLE IN NEED OF PRODUCTS OR SERVIC
THAT SOLVE A PROBLEM OR FULFIL AN EMOTIONAL NEED

AYOL HOP

Disclaimer

This e-book has been written for information purposes only. Every effort has been made to make this ebook as complete and accurate as possible. However, there may be mistakes in typography or content. Also, this ebook provides information only up to the publishing date. Therefore, this ebook should be used as a guide - not as the ultimate source. The purpose of this ebook is to educate. The author and the publisher does not warrant that the information contained in this e-book is fully complete and shall not be responsible for any errors or omissions. The author and publisher shall have neither liability nor responsibility to any person or entity with respect to any loss or damage caused or alleged to be caused directly or indirectly by this ebook.

KAYOL R. HOPE

Helping small business owners find, connect, and gain new paying customers from the web.

Visit: www.kayolhope.com

WHAT'S INSIDE...

CREATING ONLINE PRESENCE SECRETS

REQUESTING AFFILIATE APPROVAL SECRETS

FINDING QUALITY AFFILIATES SECRETS

PROMOTING AFFILIATE SECRETS

CREATING ONLINE PRESENCE SECRETS

CREATING ONLINE PRESENCE SECRETS

First impressions do count so make sure to ll out your social media profiles completely. After all, if you don't have a profile that properly represents you or your brand then how will people know what your all about? People buy from those they **Know**, **Like**, and **Trust**!

If your too lazy to ll out a simple account pro le then your people will probably see it as that and not want to do business with you.

Your profile and cover photos need to be welcoming and inviting.

* Fill in your bio
* Use your best email where people can contact you.
* Use your real name.
* Put in as much information about yourself as you can

Optimizing your profile also makes it easier for potential customers to find you searching on Google.

You do you!

No seriously, if you try and be someone or something your not then you'll fall at on your face and other people can see through people being fake or being a poser.

People love to see ing relatable human beings just like them and are often very visual. That is why many people on social media share stories and give a lifestyle sneak peak through photos. Posting pictures when you dine out is just one way of tapping into this.

Whatever you convey needs to represent what you and your brand stands for and if what you publish goes outside of those values then it will kill any traction in growing an audience.

Never post a link to your capture page or any affiliate offer on your Facebook published posts or images, until after the post starts getting engagement. Social Media websites such as Facebook actually automatically penalizes your reach when you place links on your posts. The reason is that traffic to external websites takes traffic away organically when that is the purpose of Facebook paid ads which is a big source of income.

A clever secret to get around this is to edit your post and slip and insert your ink to a capture page or affiliate offer after waiting until your post gets around 2-3 likes and comments. This allows you to build up engagement then maximize it.

Influencers are the new Celebrities and Social Media is often an outlet to be entertained. Lets face it, most people's lives are so dull and boring so if you can provide some inspiration or motivation than people with the same ideal mindset will gravitate to your content.

A secret I use is to build up my social media accounts is to post quotes from leaders in and around my niche.

A free tool I use is QuotesCover.com - https://quotescover.com/ It takes all the techie part out of creating engaging images.

Search a major search engine for a leader in your industry...

or

the search term **Motivational Speakers** and a list of results such as this should appear:

ttps://www.google.com/search?q=m

motivational speakers

All Videos Images New

Motivational speakers

Source:

https://www.instagram.com/kayolhope2/

Eric Thomas

Tony Robbins

Copy and paste the quote with credit and choose an attractive background image for the viral content.

This tool is invaluable because it allows you to and existing popular quotes that you can post for viral content perfectly formatted to various social media platforms. Instagram, Facebook, you name it.

Check out some examples I've created and published on my personal Instagram account:

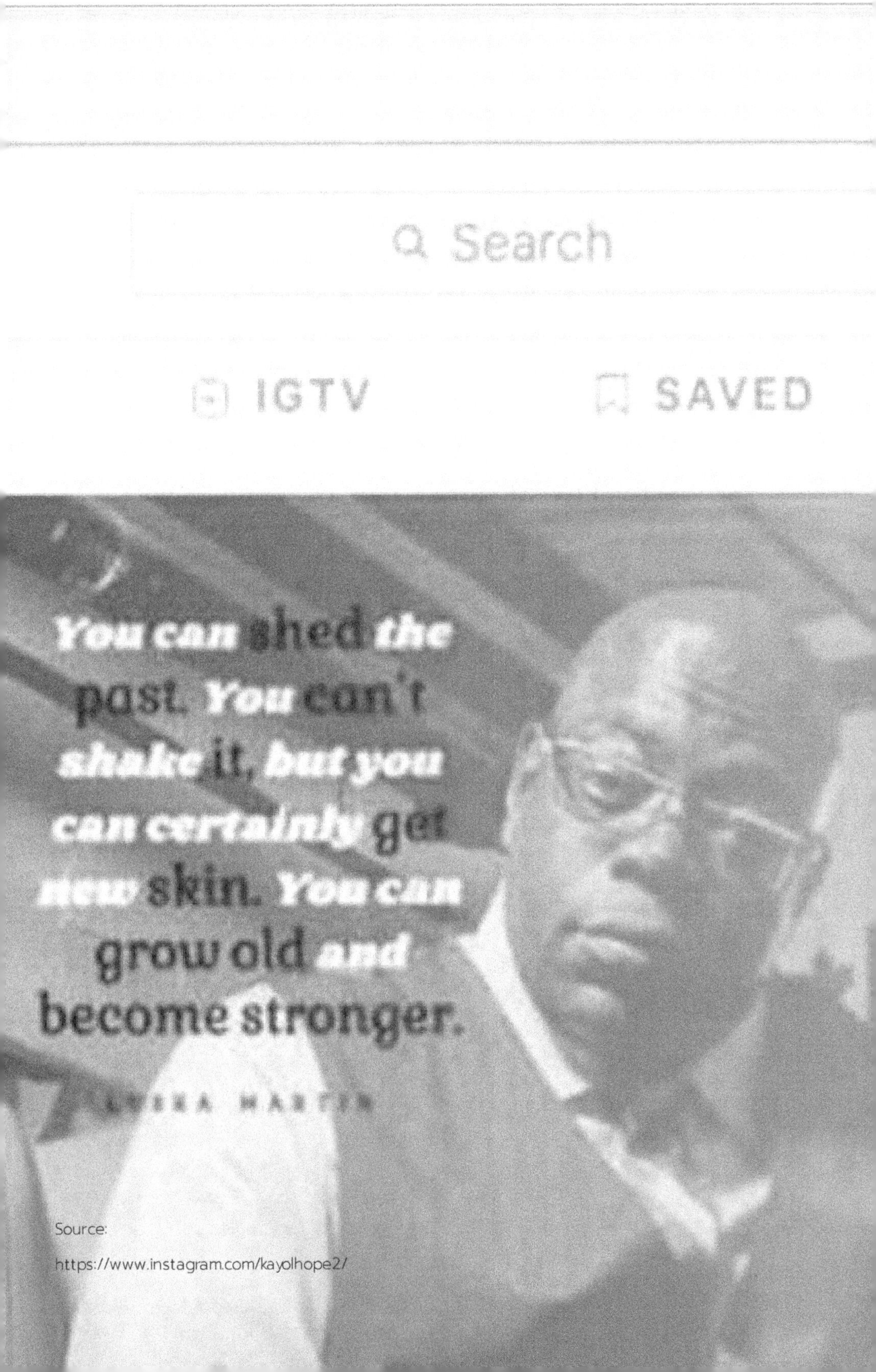

Search

IGTV

SAVED

You can shed the past. You can't shake it, but you can certainly get new skin. You can grow old and become stronger.

Source:

https://www.instagram.com/kayolhope2/

I also tend to switch things up by posting 3 or 4 of these types of posts before putting a video post or promotional type post. I feel this allows balance things and is close to the 80/20 rule for those that are familiar with that.

Source:

https://www.instagram.com/kayolhope2/

The secret is using the B-Day method. In Facebook if you search for , "Birthdays" you can get a list of all your Facebook friends that have a Birthday that day or one coming up.

You want to build a relationship without being salesy or pushy. Facebook gives you the perfect opportunity to do just that!

If write reach out to them with a personal message wishing them a Happy Birthday then generally they appreciate that you took the time to think of them and may inquire as to what you are working on or happening in your life. This how to connect with them and Facebook tends to show your posts to those you interact with on a regular basis. After all, social media is intended to allow people to connect with one another.

Here is an example:

birthdays this month

Posts People Pho

ur Groups and Pages

blic

oose a Source...

TYPE

Posts

sts You've Seen

D IN GROUP

y group

ur Groups

Birthd

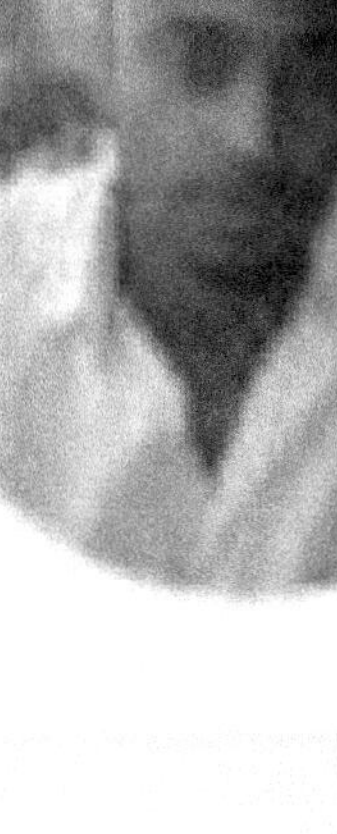

Source:

https://www.facebook.com/kayolhope

Birthdays

Happy BDay Joao Varela hope you

View Friendship

Jonathan Hamon

Happy Birthday Jonathan Hamon.

View Friendship

Source:

https://www.facebook.com/kayolhope

The next secret to driving traffic and engagement is by harnessing the power of video!

No, no, no you doesn't have to get on camera... although that can do great. Keep in mind if you would like to that almost nobody cares.

Source: The Big Bang Theory

Go to a video site such as Youtube.com or ViralVideos.com and thats just to name a couple. Look for a video related to your niche and if it is something that is trending or has over 200,000 views than download it using a free web tool such as:

KeepVid - https://keepvid.com/

Then re-upload it or edit it or even outsource someone else to repurpose the content into something new and exciting.

People are more likely to share if there is no link so wait for people to Like and Share it before sneaking in your capture page link.

Always cloak or mask affiliate links, that isn't a secret it is just smart marketing.

Nobody wants to see those long ugly links all hanging out there for the all of the Interwebs to see. Nobody needs to see that part of your business so keep it to yourself.

Speaking of ugly links you DO want to be using hashtags on certain social media platforms such as Instagram to drive relevant traffic c and while Facebook does allow the use of Hashtags just don't. It is a big faux pas.

Personally, you can search for a list of the best hangtags to use related to your niche through a built in social media software tool or using free tools such as:

Best Hashtag - http://best-hashtags.com/

Nothing beats Social Proof!

Share your income proof isn't about showing off. In fact, those in the network marketing niches waving around bank notes like a fan or showing off expensive jewelry and fancy cars should especially take a page outta my playbook. You know, because you'd never post those videos on a weekday rather then on a weekend after getting off work at your real J.O.B *(Just Over Broke)* before hitting the ATM.

It isn't about big or small amounts of income that counts but showing prove that making money online is possible. It is about being proud to show how many people you helped and in the process are that much further in reaching your own goals of success.

Too many people are all about the wrong things such as having expensive things to impress people with stuff that don't really make them happy or that people really care about.

Too many people are all talk and documented proof beats conversation every time.

When I post social proof I make sure the screenshot is published the day of or prior days earnings. I also make sure it has my username logged in with the current time and date of my computer of mobile device as too many people easily fake screenshots of unrealistic earnings in income proof screenshots by posting of someone else's income proof, old sales reports ands/or product launch earnings, etc.

My method ensues solid proof and accountability. I also post these sparingly to inspire and motivate my audience instead of bragging.

When you approach things from this angle you turn heads and people take notice be it the posers, wannabe gurus, or even the nay sayers. This gets massive engagement and helps snowball traffic c and sales.

Here is an example of an photo album I've created on FB which I keep adding and getting new eyeballs all the time:

Proof of Sales

ought that talking about money was
ealize some people have never made
been at...

See More

31 posts ·

Source:

https://www.facebook.com/kayolhope

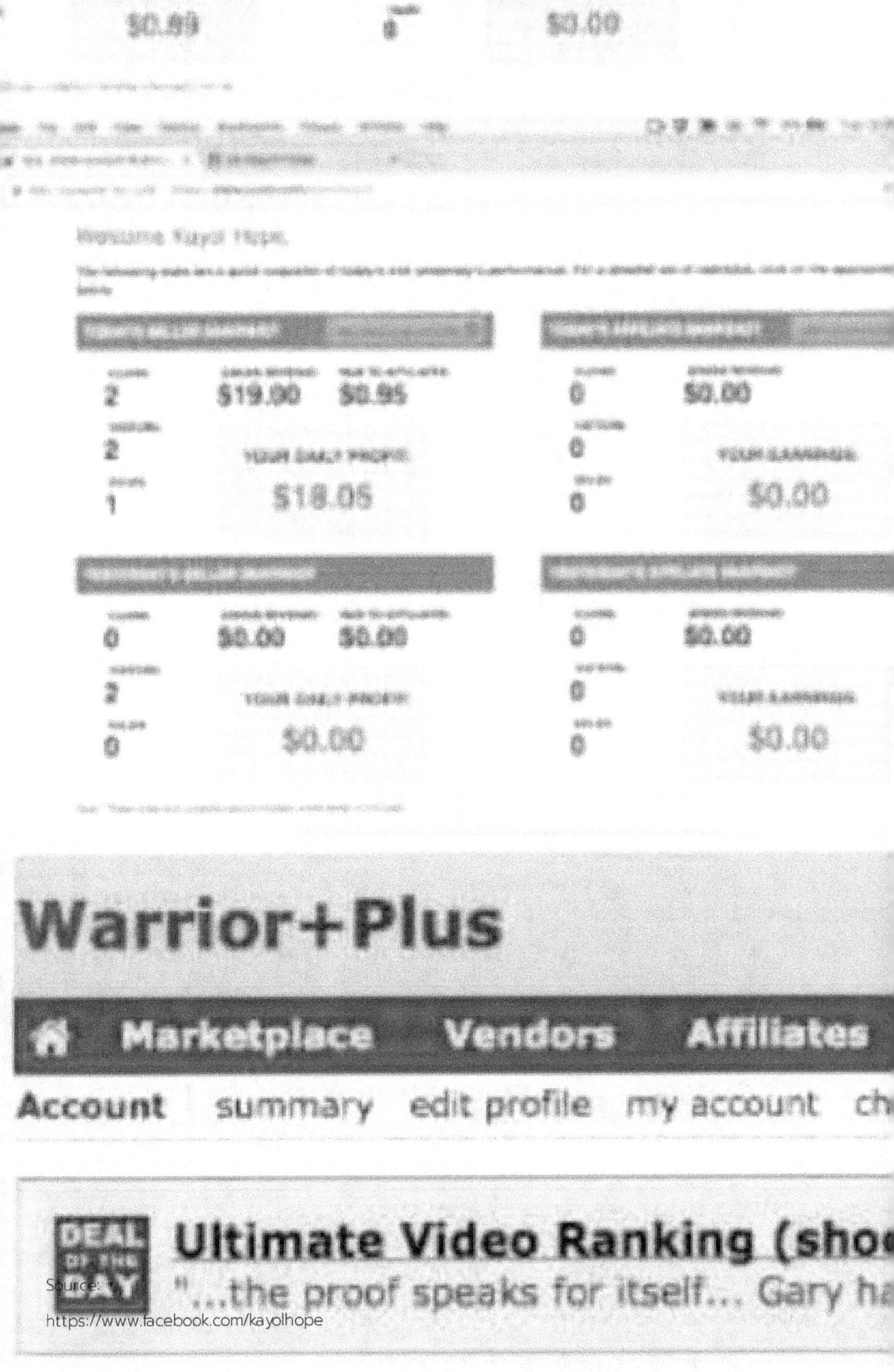

Source:
https://www.facebook.com/kayolhope

Source:

https://www.facebook.com/kayolhope

fiverr

Source:

https://www.facebook.com/kayolhope

DATE	FOR	
Feb 06, 19	CLEARING	Funds Pending Cl
Jan 31, 19	CLEARING	Funds Pending Cl
Jan 25, 19	CLEARING	Funds Pending Cl

You, Lisa Justason, Neil Bosley

Love

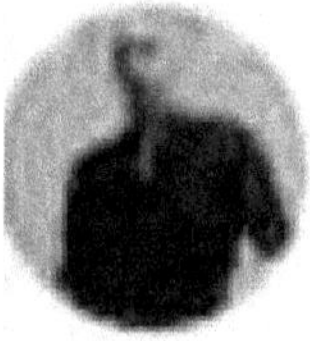

Kayol R Hope First They Igno
shut that hoopla down! Serio
that it is possible to mak... Se

Source: https://www.facebook.com/kayolhope

Consistency is key to success!

You need to keep engaging and interacting with your audience to keep it growing or your audience will leave and seek what they need elsewhere.

As in any relationship be it online or offline building an audience takes time and nurturing. You kinda have to treat it like dating. Hear me out now. You wouldn't go up to someone you just met and ask them out right? You typically would get to know that person and see if both are the right t. The same logic can be applied to marketing and think of presenting the link to your offer like proposing. You typically wouldn't pop the question unless your con dent the person is going to say, "yes".

Make sure you match the right product or service with the right target audience and have confidence your audience will say, "yes" to your offer.

REQUESTING AFFILIATE APPROVAL SECRETS

REQUESTING AFFILIATE APPROVAL SECRETS

The amount of wannabe affiliate marketers with no real track record or credibility requesting affiliate approval with free review access and instant commission is astounding.

As both an product vendor and affiliate for various online marketplaces such as JVZoo, W+, Clickbank, and more I can tell you while stats of a potential affiliate being approved or not is taken into consideration I've learned that all vendors want is to feel that affiliates will promote ethically and put a solid effort in. Understand that vendors take all the risk especially when it comes to traffic methods and repeat refunders that destroy the success of a product launch.

That is why I personally consider the amount of sales and duration of time a potential affiliate has been a member of one of these platforms. Any less then 25 sales and less than 3 months is a good rule of thumb for me.

Everyone has to start somewhere though so often I will grant approval on delayed commission until the affiliate proves themselves by earning trust and sales. This is also the affiliate secret I've personally used to gain approval for big new launches. Even when the vendor has already told me, "No"!

Here is an example of a request not just for affiliate access to Mike Thomas better known as Mike from Maine and a well-known and highly respected affiliate and product reviewer of Internet Marketing products online but... product review access with very few previous affiliate sales.

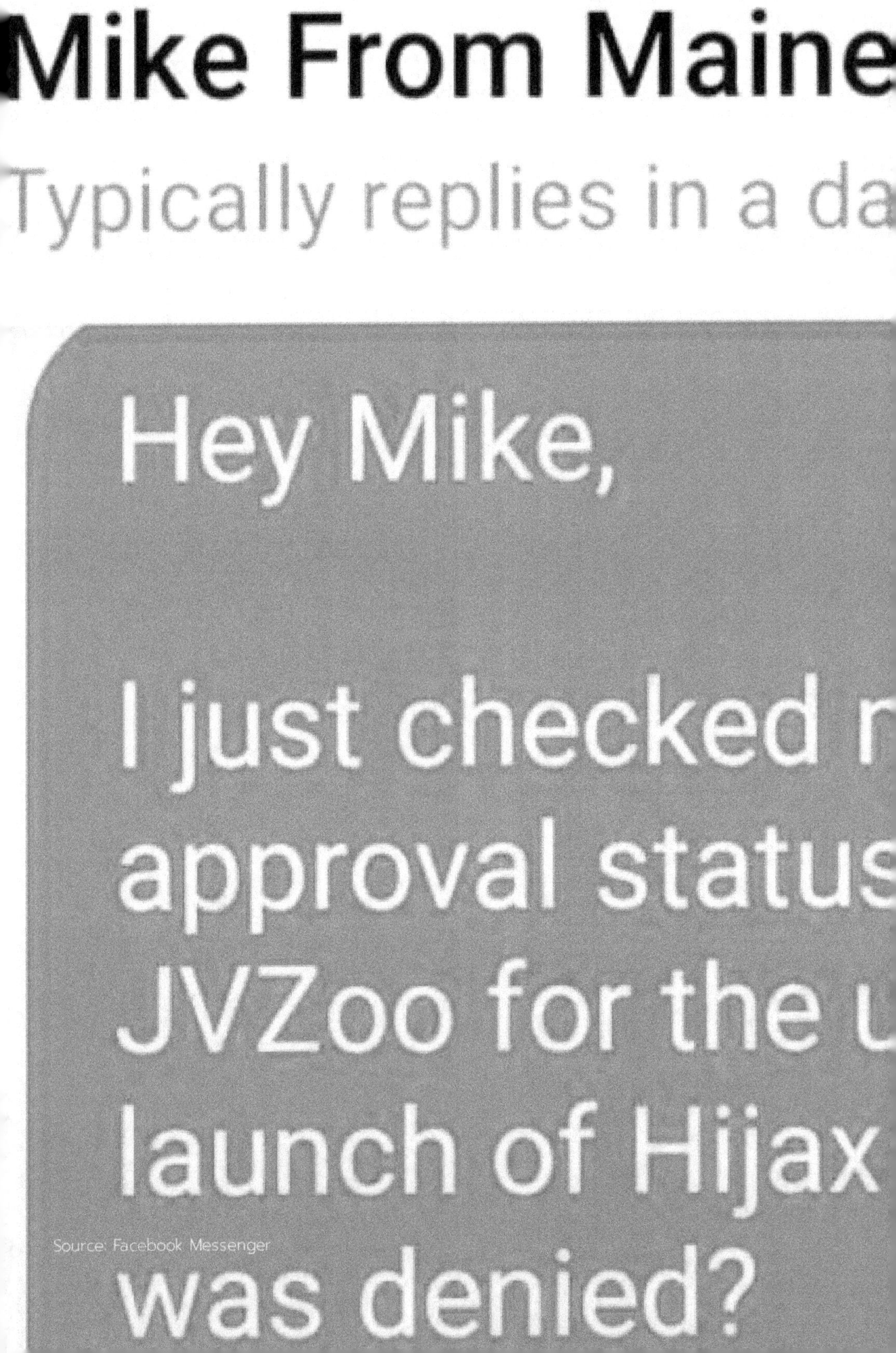

Mike From Maine

Typically replies in a da

Hey Mike,

I just checked r
approval status
JVZoo for the u
launch of Hijax
was denied?

Source: Facebook Messenger

it is due to lack o
ell I mentioned th
e glad to be set to
order to build sa
ust. Waiting out t
eriod eliminates a
ou guys while it gi
filiates like mysel
nance.

Source: Facebook Messenger

yet
cat
nee
but
unl

JAN. 2

Source: Facebook Messenger

ok approv

Here is the full chat transcript:

Me: Hey Mike,

I just checked my affiliate approval status over on JVZoo for the upcoming launch of Hijax and see I was denied?

I've connected with you and Brett Rutecky through social media and have bought through you guys on a regular basis.

If it is due to lack of sales, well I mentioned that I would be glad to be set to delayed in order to build sales and trust. Waiting out the refund period eliminates any risk to you guys while it gives affiliates like myself a chance.

I've followed all the training yet it still seems to be a catch 22 situation of you need sales to be approved but you can't make sales unless you get approved?

Mike from Maine: ok approved

Me: Thank you, I really appreciate that.

Okay, so you got approval to promote as an affiliate right?

Good well if not make plugging away as someone is bound to give you a chance so stay humble and remain hungry!

FINDING QUALITY AFFILIATES SECRETS

FINDING QUALITY AFFILIATES SECRETS

It only takes a handful of super affiliates to put any product launch over the top!

The secret to finding quality affiliates is <u>NOT</u> in big extravagant JV (Junior Venture) contests... na, that is mostly for show and somewhat incestuous in nature which you may want to avoid unless your into that circle jerking kind of behaviour. Too much, "I'll promote your launch, if you promote ours". Blah, blah, blah.

al symbol for
iprocate hard

Source: Kayol Hope

The secret of finding the right affiliates to promote for you is seeking them out through social media, top leader boards, and so on. You contact them with a great product launch and you let them know just wants in it for them!

You find them by contacting in influencers in your niche through social media and requesting a shoutout.

You can easily tap into the audience of Instagram users with large accounts. Many major accounts will allow you to pay them for getting your offer in front of their audience.

This is the ideal method for growing an audience quickly while avoiding costly paid ad cost and fake follower bots.

Pay it forward by Liking and commenting on other people's content since many people are curious to find out about the audience they are growing. They may just do the same for you. Give without expecting anything in return and you will never be disappointed but grateful when you are rewarded.

PROMOTING AFFILIATE SECRETS

PROMOTING AFFILIATE SECRETS

Promote only products that you have a true understanding and working knowledge behind. Either get a review copy to test or invest before promoting.

The first secret method for promoting affiliate offers is to seek those looking for help and have a problem that your offer solves. If you search on **Quora** or other forums related to your niche you will find people struggling with something. You can also apply this method to **Facebook** groups related to your niche.

Maybe it is driving traffic or converting that traffic to sales. Perhaps a unknown method such as the ones you discover in this ebook solve that issue? Perhaps a new page builder will help give the stunning call-to- action needed to close sales and resolve a conversion issue?

In fact, if you have a **Twitter** account you can search for phases such as, *"How to get more traffic?"* and you will get all the search results of those seeking out an answer for a solution to a problem you have the answer to. While your affiliate link maybe the solution be sure to private message them and get them warmed up to you before pitching.

Are you frustrated at not having the online success you had hoped for?

Seeing others achieve their goals (and more)? Well, don't be despondent anymore as finally you are going to discover how others are achieving online success and financial freedom.

Here's the secret it's implementing a proven strategy that top business people use and can be applied to any project.

You see

After much studying it's been discovered that it's possible to identify niches that have the very best chance of success and more important how to find them. It took time and many hours of research but gradually pro table opportunities appeared that had literally been hidden in plain sight. Profits like:

$50,000 $100,00 Even **$200,000**

a year and what's great is anyone can make use of this strategy! You just need to realize the value of information that is right in front of you – 'hidden in plain sight!'

Only when you start looking do you realize how entrepreneurs are quietly using this strategy to give themselves a huge advantage over everybody else. You see it's a bit like following a trail of breadcrumbs (information) which once correctly identified and activated sets you up to earn a regular monthly income or a big pile of cash in one payment!

Now over time a system has been developed and fine-tuned which seeks out proven niches where success is virtually guaranteed. This high level information can if wanted also be used for consultancy work. Advise clients using this 'inside knowledge', and for similar success. Do not worry it's all perfectly legal; I wouldn't want it any other way.

This system can be used to 'look into the future' and see the potential of projects. Then push the 'GO button' if everything lines up or walk away because the system says 'NO'. It's just like having a crystal ball! .... This tried and tested plan cuts out the 'no pie in the sky ideas' with little time and no money wasted on them, don't you hate wasting time?

You see time has a value like money and the more time you have for the valuable things in life like being with family or spending out on luxuries like rest and relaxation the better.

So through trial and error this system has been developed that can be used on any potential online or offline project to know in advance whether it has the potential of making money and so pursue it or totally avoid. It starts with a secret that is literally hidden in plain sight and from there you can see immediately whether to hit the green for go or red for no. This system has done away with many frustrating failures....

But tell me this are you frustrated because you like the idea of having your own business and making money online... ...but struggle to get anything off the ground...and you always end up with nothing to show? Well I'm here to tell you it's not your fault. The cards are stacked against you and it's because you don't have a proven plan that works.

Full PLR rights are part of your package so not only can you read and learn the techniques but you can edit the reports, sell them as articles, content or blog posts. The choice is yours....

Now you might be thinking why reveal this plan, wouldn't it make more sense to keep it secret? The simple answer is there are so many opportunities to find using this system it's not possible to keep up with all of them. There's a never ending stream, it's the strategy that just keeps on giving! As mentioned there are so many niches to pro t from with your purchase full PLR rights are included which means you can sell these products onto other entrepreneurs and earn money.

straight away so everyone gets the benefit. Happy Days all round! Here's a few suggestions how to reuse the text:

* Create your own e book,
* Content for a blog
* Turn into a press release
* Use in a number of articles
* Make a video with screenshots

You literally just have to decide how to profit from this solid information.

Forget over-hyped here today gone tomorrow Facebook strategies, SEO, Instagram or Pinterest reliant ideas. This is a rock solid time proven system that will be here for years to come..

It's your opportunity to earn regular weekly and monthly income or the option to have a lump sum cash payout (if that's what you prefer). Take control of your life now and experience the freedom of working from in a niche that you will love!

Okay, okay... check out this exclusive opportunity below:

Tired of Building Someone Else's Dreams?
http://ivpages.net/show/5497/

www.ingramcontent.com/pod-product-compliance
Lightning Source LLC
Chambersburg PA
CBHW070948200526
45161CB00001BA/29

9780359767410